MW00533642

SoaringME

Guide to

Successful Salary

Negotiation…

Published by Ethical Recruiters, Inc. DBA SoaringME

ISBN-13: 978-1-956874-00-6

Table of Contents

Visit

SoaringME.com

for more resources.

Preface

Dear Reader,

This book is the result of thousands of salary negotiations that have taken place since I began my career in recruiting back in 1997. I have had the pleasure of working with tens of thousands of fantastic candidates and employers, I have learned something from every one of them.

Throughout the years I have negotiated hourly rate, salary, annual bonus, sign-on bonuses, relocation packages, vacation time, work schedule, holiday pay, job titles, job responsibilities, preemptive severance packages, educational reimbursement, early performance review, and various forms of equity in the company. All these negotiations are slightly different, but the successful negotiations have a lot in common with one another. The candidates' approach to how they negotiated with their employer or the company offering them employment was the key to their success.

Best of luck, and I hope that you get the compensation package that you're going after!

M. L. Miller

Founder, SoaringME

Introduction

Negotiation is a skill that anyone can learn, practice, and improve upon. Hence, this book has been created to give job seekers the confidence needed to obtain the best possible terms. It contains salary negotiation tactics and techniques that lead to the most successful outcomes.

A good negotiation is a process, not an event or meeting where you sit down in an adversarial struggle to get the other side to give you something in some confrontational way.

If you are reading this book, you are likely preparing for a job search, or asking your current company for a raise.

This book is written plainly with easy-to-follow advice that will make your salary negotiations more successful. There is a process to achieving a successful salary negation and I have mapped it out in the following pages.

The most successful techniques in negotiating salary are not adversarial because the people negotiating might end up working together. Maintaining a good relationship between employee and employer is part of what will make your negotiation successful. The most effective negotiators that I have dealt with never create a hostile or combative situation to achieve their objectives.

It is important for you to understand not only what your own priorities are, but also to understand what the priorities of the employer are. This way you have all the information and can proceed with your negotiation accordingly.

Market conditions have an enormous influence on compensation negotiations. When a talent market is very tight, meaning that the supply of talent is not great enough to meet the demand for that talent, then the employers are much more willing to concede in a negotiation. If the opposite is true, and the supply of talent exceeds the demand for that talent, then employers are much less willing to concede. Therefore, salaries rise for highly specialized talent, and that is why it is to your benefit to consider negotiating to build your skills too.

The advice given here is based on decades of experience, negotiating thousands of compensation packages. Take advantage of all the information in this book as everything here will help you achieve your goals for negotiation of the terms of employment.

Most Candidates Do Not Negotiate

Most people do not negotiate salaries very often in their career, so it is understandable that many of them are intimidated about the process. There have been multiple surveys conducted about negotiating compensation. The findings reveal that over half of the candidates do not negotiate at all, as much as seventy-five percent in some surveys, and in my experience this is accurate. The data shows that older candidates negotiate more often than younger ones, this is due to more experience and confidence. The studies also show that men negotiate their job offers more often than women do.

While at the same time, most employers are willing to

negotiate. Even in a candidate-driven market, when recruiters and hiring managers almost expect a job offer to be negotiated, most candidates still do not. Confidence is the key to a successful negotiation, and preparation is the key to confidence. The more preparation you do before you enter the interview process, the better off you will be.

Start by recognizing that we do not see your attempt to negotiate your compensation as a bad thing. Being somebody who has been personally responsible for thousands of salary negotiations, I have never been offended or upset by the fact that a candidate counters an offer. However, I have been concerned with the way some candidates have tried to negotiate.

Mistakes to Avoid

These are candidate behaviors that often lead to failed negotiations. There is a point at which the employer sees their best option as going to their backup candidate and moving on. There are a lot of self-proclaimed experts online who give worthless advice on negotiating. Their advice usually promotes the idea of playing games with your prospective employer. Unless the company is wanting to hire someone who acts like that in the new job, playing games is not a winning strategy for you.

Taking a win-lose approach:

- Having an over-inflated view of your market value.

- Having an under-inflated view of your market value.

- Failing to ask for something that is important to you.
- Using a pretend or even real job offer as a weapon in the negotiation.
- Negotiating simply for the sake of negotiating.

Things like not being the first one to speak, making absurd asks, or being evasive when the recruiter is asking you about your expectations are all examples of what not to do. You want to go in confidently and with a plan, but you do not want to ruin it for yourself either.

In my experience these are the types of candidates who think if they follow some template or trending technique then they will "win" their negotiation. Trying to control the situation or turning every question around onto the other side are things that can be perceived as anything from *"This person isn't very professional and might represent our company poorly"* to a red flag of a possible problem employee if we hire them. You should be cautious about following any advice that wants you to play hardball.

Taking the approach that negotiating is a zero-sum game is the most common mistake that I see candidates make. I've had many discussions with hiring managers and Human Resources representatives about questions they have after seeing these tactics. They wonder if these candidates have the personality that they want to hire.

Real World Examples

Over the course of my career, I have experienced some candidates who have provided good examples of what you should not do.

I recall working with a sales representative who was still early in their career. At the beginning of the process, I asked about their compensation expectations and the candidate stated that they wanted to do some more research before giving me an answer. This candidate along with others went through several steps of the interview process until a close decision was made to move this one to final interviews. For the second time I asked this candidate for their expectations, and again they avoided giving me an answer. They told me that there were one or two more people that they wanted to speak to prior to discussing it with me. This put me and the hiring manager in a difficult position because it would look bad for both of us if the candidate completed the final interviews but wanted much more than the budget allowed. Plus, we began to have questions about the candidates coachability, and ethics. What the candidate did not consider is that the second-place candidate was a strong backup choice and so we moved forward with the other candidate, and they ended up getting the job. The first-choice candidate lost out on the opportunity simply by playing games.

Another time, I worked with a Senior Director level candidate who initially told me that their current compensation was in the mid-200,000's, which meant to me that they were currently making around 250K. At the end of the interview process, this candidate was preferred over one other who was also very strong. As I talked to the candidate again about their compensation expectations, I knew at that point that 270K was the maximum that the company would pay for the base salary. The candidate informed me that they double-checked their current base salary, and it was 262,500. Then, the candidate informed me that their expectation was 300K at a minimum for what it would take in salary for them to accept an offer. Of course, this was a remedial attempt to "high-ball" me in hopes of negotiating the best offer they could. The problem was that the role they were interviewing for would involve some negotiating on behalf of the company, and the candidate wasn't doing a good job at it. Plus, we had a strong backup candidate. Naturally I knew that we could negotiate with this candidate to try to finalize a deal. The vast majority of hiring managers I had worked with in the past have taken these tactics as a sign that the candidate was not the best person for the job. However, I had forgotten that the candidate was a professional acquaintance of the hiring manager. I was asked to extend the offer for the maximum amount and let the candidate know that it was the best and final offer. The candidate accepted and avoided losing the opportunity despite their poor negotiation tactics. But how many of you have a strong enough connection with the hiring manager to save you from this type of mistake?

Regardless of how high or low the figures involved are, there is not a technique or tactic that will guarantee your success in negotiating, and even very few that will guarantee failure. Approach your negotiations with the idea of doing the things that increase your odds of success and avoiding the mistakes that decrease those odds.

Various Agendas

When it comes to interviewing and negotiating to fill a role, each person involved has their own values and agenda. Below are the various perspectives of the parties involved and what you need to know going in.

The Outside Recruiters' Perspective.

Salary negotiation is something that should begin before you ever have your first conversation with the recruiter. Prior to interviewing with an outside recruiter, you should have a preliminary idea of what the market-rate is for a candidate in your position.

As a professional Executive Recruiter, or what many

refer to as a "Headhunter", I always bring up compensation as early as possible in my interaction with a candidate. Having a conversation about money expectations allows me to learn how serious the candidate is, how realistic they are about their value on the market, and how flexible they might be if a job offer is presented to them. My objective is to have you accept an offer that you are going to be happy with now and for many years to come. A good recruiter simply wants to make sure that both sides are thinking along the same lines. You will also learn some of the most current salary data from the outside recruiter.

The Corporate Recruiters' Perspective.

The main things that influence the approach of the in-house recruiter in salary negotiations are the current market for candidates of your level, the growth happening at the company, the urgency of that open position, and your performance in the interview process.

Corporate recruiters will often speak to candidates about their salary expectation in their first interaction. The better ones will be transparent about the budget or salary range for the position you are interviewing for.

Creating value that separates you from the other candidates will have the greatest impact on your success of negotiating a good compensation package. In most organizations, the talent acquisition team is essentially a service department to help hiring managers within the company fill their open positions. Corporate recruiters are highly motivated to hire the candidates that their internal clients really want. Most talent acquisition professionals do not see negotiation as an adversarial event, but simply part of the process and what they need to do to fill the position.

The Hiring Managers' Perspective.

The hiring manager has a set of goals that they are accountable for and are typically hiring someone because they need that person to achieve those goals. If during the interview process the candidate demonstrates that they would be an outstanding contributor to the hiring managers' success, then they become very motivated to bring that candidate onto their team. But if the job applicant gives the impression that they would be an average or slightly above average employee, then the hiring manager is less likely to stretch compensation too far.

A successful negotiation will be based on you creating value in yourself by having strong, successful interviews. Read my book *SoaringME The Ultimate Guide to Successful Job Interviewing* to learn how to create the most value during the interview process.

The Human Resource Departments' Perspective.

When an employer makes a job offer, either orally or in writing, they typically provide a compensation package that includes a base salary or hourly wage alongside a benefits package, and sometimes an expense account and/or some form of equity in the company.

Employers vary quite a bit on compensation, usually having to do with where they are at in their lifecycle as an organization. Startup companies are more likely to be modest in the cash portions of their compensation packages because they are often pre-revenue, and they try to attract talent with equity (Restricted Stock Units or Stock Options with the potential of a high upside). More established companies may still have an equity component to their compensation, but their stock prices are typically more stable, and they can afford to be more competitive on the cash side, such as base salary, relocation packages, and sign-on bonuses.

To stay competitive with what the marketplace is paying, many companies will purchase data from salary survey companies. They may also have a compensation expert working within HR, or they could hire a compensation consultant.

Human Resources departments in more established companies usually have instituted a system that tries to keep employees in similar levels of jobs at an even pay scale. They are trying to avoid problems with employee morale that would occur if one employee discovered that another employee is in a position of nearly equal responsibility, with equal experience and education and is making twenty-five to thirty percent more in salary. Systems like these can have a big impact on salary negotiations. If the job candidate is asking for that twenty-five to thirty percent above what the company is already paying employees at a similar level, it is unlikely to be a successful negotiation. However, if the candidate is so exceptional, they might consider adding additional responsibilities to the job and making it a higher-level position.

The Job Candidate.

The job candidate may choose to bargain for more pay if he/she believes that the offer is not commensurate with their professional qualifications, skills, and academic achievements.

There are a lot of processes involved in negotiating an exceptional job offer. But negotiating offers vary from one organization to another. Not everybody needs to negotiate their salary or pay, but several studies have shown that those who chose to negotiate do earn more than those who do not.

Some people look at the experience they will gain from working at a job as more valuable than the rate they are paid, because in the long run that experience may increase their earnings even more. If a job candidate decides that they want to maximize their earnings on a particular job to offer their services, following the steps in the next chapter increases the chances of a successful negotiation.

Steps to Success in Salary Negotiation

Gather Market Intelligence.

The most critical step in successful salary negation begins before you apply for the job and continues through the interview process. You should begin with online searches for salary ranges of employees with your credentials, in your geography and line of work. Your research online should include multiple websites that provide this type of information. At the time of writing this book, my suggestion is to use GlassDoor.com and Salary.com but please realize that employers use other data from paid salary survey companies.

The data collected by these websites can be out of date from what is currently being paid in the market, but they are more accurate than government data. Increasingly companies are including pay ranges on their job postings, and I expect that to increase as many States will be requiring this information. Even if a job posting lists a maximum pay for the position, I suspect most will have some flexibility for a strong candidate who does well in the interview process. You obviously do not want to undersell your value, but you also do not want to overshoot. Reaching out to known contacts within the same field can also provide you with compensation insights. These sources may not be precisely accurate, but they will give a general idea of what to expect.

It is important that you learn what you can about what the company typically pays employees with similar experience and education, for similar roles and level.

You also should research what their competitors pay employees, using the same criteria. The more sources you research the more accurate your numbers will be, but you should disregard any wildly low or high figures.

After gathering some preliminary data about market rates, you will be ready to apply for the position and have a conversation with the recruiter. Speaking with recruiters will give you the most current information on salaries being paid. The recruiter will want to discuss compensation to know if there is a reasonable chance that both you and the employer will be able to agree.

It is important that you also do your research on relocation and cost of living in the area at where the job is situated if it is not where you currently reside. Relocating to an area that is more affordable, or more expensive will require adjustments to your salary expectations.

Determine What is Most Important to You, and to The Company.

As mentioned earlier, the most valuable thing gained from working a job may be the experience itself. In the long run, this experience may provide more career fulfillment and more earnings potential. Other things to consider would be working remotely, negotiating a favorable work schedule, and responsibilities. I have worked with employers who were willing to negotiating the reimbursement of continuing education and training, a severance package written into the employment contract because the company had financial uncertainties, even an early performance review with a salary increase so that the candidate could prove their worth and then have a salary increase after three or six months.

Some candidates negotiate to have fewer responsibilities on a job if they feel that would be more in-line with the pay being offered. Others may want to negotiate having more responsibilities on a job so they can gain that experience and list it on their resume moving forward.

Additional responsibilities could allow you to channel that experience into a better job in the future with higher pay. There are many things to look for and examine besides salary that you should be able to negotiate depending on how much value you create.

Choose Your Negotiating Style.

Generally, there are five main styles of negotiation:

- **Accommodating.** (Trying the make the other side happy by giving them what they want.)

- **Compromising.** (Trying to achieve half of what you ask for and giving the other side half of what they ask for.)

- **Avoiding.** (Avoiding confrontation by not bringing up concerns or objections.)

- **Competitive.** (Trying to win a victory against the other side.)

- **Collaborating.** (Trying to work together with the other side to create a win/win agreement.)

The accommodating, compromising, and avoiding styles do not result in higher compensation, and should be avoided. Accommodating is the best approach to allow the other side to walk all over you. This leads to being unhappy with the results, and usually damages the relationship in the end. Compromising sounds good, but it does not prioritize what is most important to each side, it simply goes for half. This leaves important wants unfulfilled for one or both of the parties. The avoiding style of negotiating creates dissatisfaction and resentment which leads to a bad working relationship. Competitive negotiating may result in higher compensation, but regardless of the amount of the increase, the people who use this style are usually unhappy because they wanted a bigger win. This style of negotiating creates a "win-lose" mentality and that damages the relationship with the new employer. Collaborating is the ideal negotiation style.

To achieve a "win-win" between both parties, you should follow the collaborating negotiation style. This type of negotiation realizes that the relationship between the employer and employee is a valuable part of what should be considered. To achieve the collaborating style, you should develop criteria for different solutions that you could say *"yes"* to. But, before offering any solution, you should learn what is important to the employer. For instance, assume that you begin to negotiate after you receive an offer for a job. There would be set of objectives for you and the employer, and after some discussion, you both agree that there is a certain solution that fulfills all objectives of both the employer and for you too. It becomes a "win-win" because it gets to a stage where both the employer and you as the employee reach a common agreement. Both sides work together to understand what is valued by each of you, and then find a solution that satisfies both, hence the negotiation is considered collaborative.

Plan the Best Time to Initiate Negotiations.

It is a big mistake to try to negotiate too early, or too late. From the beginning there is some pre-negotiation that happens as you are expressing your salary expectations, and the recruiter is divulging their salary range. But the optimal time to bring up your desire to negotiate is when the offer is being made. Before accepting, it is fine to request a day or two to consider the offer or you can make a counter offer right on the spot. In a new job situation, the only time that you should mention your salary expectations is when the employer asks.

Never bring it up on your own! So, it could be right at the beginning, it could be during the interview or screening process, or could be at the end when a job offer has been received but regardless, only bring up your salary expectations when prompted by the employer. Bringing it up on your own may portray you as being money-hungry, and this is not the impression you want to create.

The most professional and persuasive way you can relay your desire for a better offer is to briefly explain the value you would bring to that department and company, display knowledge of your genuine market value, and then simply explain that you were expecting the offer to be higher, or the hours to be better, or whatever your priority is. Know what your values are and be prepared to counter if the initial offer is not what you are looking for.

When you want to ask for a raise from your current employer, then you can let it be known during your performance review. This might be before the fiscal year begins or at the end because that is the period most managers expect for these discussions to happen. It is usually acceptable for you to leverage your performance results as well as your market value, it also shows that you are prepared ahead of time and have done your research. Use all of this to leverage and explain why you deserve a higher salary or paycheck.

Lead with Interest.

Before proposing any counteroffers, it is best to ensure that the person extending the job offer understands that it is appreciated and that there is sincere interest in working the job. The counteroffer should be presented as wanting the work, but with different terms.

In negotiating an offer, you should not be self-focused, rather you should examine the company's interest and show your sincere desire to help them as an employee.

The salary negotiation process has to do with communicating your economic value to an organization. It is about justifying why you are worth what you are asking for. Going in with positive intentions will help you to increase your chances of getting a positive result.

Demonstrate Your Value to The Employer.

The best offers go to the candidates who were the most impressive in the interview process. By creating value in the minds of the employer, you create the most leverage because your employment is something they want.

To justify a better offer, you want to make sure you can articulate why you are a valuable employee. For instance, when you are making a counteroffer or the company tells you that your request is outside of what they typically pay, you should be ready to remind them of your accomplishments, awards, certifications, education, etc. There is also value when you receive a competing job offer from another employer. This is something that you should let the hiring manager as well as the recruiter know. It does create a scarcity frame of mind in the employer because if they are interested in your expertise, they will be willing to pay more if they know you could be easily snatched up by someone else. Avoid doing this in a way that seems like you are playing games or being manipulative, because that will cause them to question your character.

In a situation where you are asking for a raise in your current company, then it is not necessary to bring up the fact that you have received multiple offers. Even if you had received it earlier, you could simply say, *"This is what the market is offering"* and that you are confident it is what the market offers for your level of qualifications.

You should only imply rather than saying it outright, so you do not strain the relationship with your employer. Avoid making this sound like some type of threat or ultimatum.

You want to concisely highlight your value, achievements, and accomplishments. Your aim is to prove to the employer why you are a top performer and why you stand out from everyone else. You should focus on letting them know why you are different from the others in your department, and you truly do deserve more. You can achieve this by simply saying:

"Over the past years, I've done X, Y, and Z, and if you compare me to the rest of the team, nobody else has achieved the same type of accomplishments that I have, therefore I am worth more than my current compensation."

A softer approach would be to say something along the lines of *"The market rate for someone who has successfully achieved X, Y, and Z is around $X for a base salary."*

Try pointing out the contrast between you and your team in the production, quality, and value the company receives from you.

Give a Specific Figure, not a Range.

When an employer asks, *"what are your salary expectations?"* Do not give them a range of what you expect the compensation to be. This is a terrible mistake most candidates make because employers are going to focus on your minimum figure. If you give them a range, the higher number is what you usually truly want.

You should have two numbers in mind when it comes to salary. These are your ideal amount, and then your minimum acceptable amount. Your ideal number is that highest realistic figure you can hope to expect. The minimum acceptable number is the amount that is justified and what you are worth, but anything below this figure, you will move onto another opportunity. Both numbers should be realistic compared to what the market is paying based on your research. So, when you are being asked, *"What are your salary expectations?"* You should give your ideal number, which should not be that far above the amount that you are willing to settle for. You provide this number to the employer, and they may reply with, *"Okay, we feel this role is worth $Y."* Based on your research, the number that they provide should be close to or within the range that you have in your mind. If it is below your minimum number, then you should counteroffer with that minimum figure. If it is between your two numbers, you might try one more counter, but you have already made yourself more money. This counteroffer should be something as simple as saying "I'd prefer $X."

Make Your Counteroffer/Request.

Letting the employer know that you would like a better offer does not need to be complicated. Some of the most effective approaches that I have seen candidates use were to say, *"This was not what I was expecting.", or "I was hoping/expecting the salary to be higher"* (or whatever part of *the package is most important to you).* As the one extending the offer, I typically follow statements like these up with a question to find about what they were expecting. Candidates who know what the market is paying for someone like them and have created a lot of interest from the hiring manager because they interviewed so strongly, usually have leverage. Often, they will ask for 2-3 days to consider the offer, and then come back with a counteroffer. They are willing to accept the job if they are paid a specific salary, or the equity was higher, or some other change from the original offer.

A straight-forward request from you is usually the most effective approach. Make your points using data rather than emotions. Something like "From my research, I know that XYZ, and ABC companies are paying '$X' for somebody with my skills and background." will be far more successful than something like *"I feel that I am* worth this much." or "I deserve to be paid more because I work hard." or "I'm a great employee.".

Even if you need a better schedule, it can be as simple as saying *"I have been looking at remote opportunities, and I appreciate that you are offering two work-from-home days per week, but it would work better for me if we could make that three days a week."* Or if you are early in your career and trying to build up your skills, you might simply say *"I appreciate the offer, and I know that I would be great at the job that you described. But I'm really looking to take on new responsibilities so I will accept the job and start the first of next month if we can add to the duties so that they include being trained and working on all 'X' projects."*

Whatever you include in your counteroffer, make sure that you present the evidence to justify your request and then stop. Do not negotiate with yourself by telling the employer that you open to taking something less than what you are asking for, even if you are. Just be patient. Let the employer have their internal analysis and discussions about your counteroffer. As long as they know that you are interested in working for them but are simply asking for different terms.

Give Your Commitment.

Committing to accept the job if the employer agrees to your counteroffer, is true leverage. You are far more likely to have your counteroffer accepted if you offer your commitment along with your request for better terms. This means that you should also provide your potential employer with the date that you will start the job if they accept these proposed new terms.

When communicating your counteroffer, you want to provide the information you have gathered in your research. If you uncovered that other companies offer something more to candidates with your level of experience, let the person extending the offer with you know. This is the point where you should lay your cards on the table for what your research shows is fair so that the employer has an idea of whether they can meet your expectations.

Many candidates are uncomfortable laying all their cards on the table. But this is utilizing all the research you've done and then levering your commitment to increase the success rate of your counteroffer. For instance, if you receive a job offer and you think you can get more in salary or some other aspect of the offer, you should say something like: *"I'm excited about the opportunity, but I was expecting the offer to be different/more. I will accept the job if you"* (Insert your ask here.) That should be followed by stating the start date that you commit to, if they agree to your request.

So, you are basically assuring the employer that you are not going to be playing negotiation games with them. You are accepting the company's offer for employment but on the condition that they improve their offer in a particular area to meet your expectations and what the market is paying for employees like you.

Be Flexible but Be Willing to Walk Away.

While it is important to take the wants and needs of potential new employers into consideration, there is a point at which it makes sense to walk away from any offer. There are many things to consider when determining what the walk away point is. What are your alternatives? How reasonable is your counteroffer? Does the employer have a strong backup candidate in the interview process? Do not let your pride or emotion make this decision for you. Ideally, before you begin negotiating you should not only know what is most important to you, but also at what level you would be better off to decline the offer and choose an alternative.

Summary.

The above techniques are tested and proven to work for any industry in negotiating compensation. The reality is that one should never be afraid to negotiate their pay or make a counteroffer, since the odds are very low that you will lose anything. Getting more money or benefits is sometimes as simple as asking!

However, it is critical to negotiate a compensation and benefits package that matches your needs while still being competitive with industry norms.

Many employers think that salary negotiations are part of the process, they are perfectly okay with it, so don't be afraid to engage with them. Most organizations anticipate it, but most job candidates are hesitant to do so.

In the end, working a job is going to be about gaining valuable new experience while selling your labor for as much as possible. It is not always beneficial to lose the opportunity to gain valuable experience over a small amount of money in the short-term. If it makes sense to negotiate for a better offer, following the steps in this chapter will lead to getting the best results.

Here is a quick reference summary of the steps you should take when you are negotiating your compensation:

1. Gather market intelligence.
2. Determine what is most important to you and to the company.
3. Choose your negotiating style.
4. Plan the best time to initiate negotiations.
5. Lead with interest.
6. Demonstrate your value to the employer.

7. Give a specific figure, not a range.
8. Make your counteroffer/request.
9. Give your commitment.
10. Be flexible but be willing to walk away.

Conclusion

The success of a salary negotiation happens well before the actual negotiation itself. Getting a worthy deal is about doing your research, understanding what the market rates are, and realistically what the value is for a candidate just like you. The employer has very little leverage with a candidate who knows what the market is paying and has shown an enormous amount of value during the interview process.

Successful negotiations also rely on you understanding what is most important to you. Is it salary, bonus, equity, time off, gaining experience and building your resume? Is it a robust benefits package? College reimbursement? A candidate who is early in their career will be better served in the long run by negotiating more responsibilities that they can then leverage for more pay in future negotiations. Candidates that have a solid understanding of what their market value is, and what they want, are far more successful in negotiating.

Ultimately you must think about what you are trying to accomplish by accepting this job, and what your alternatives are. You will need to know what your bottom line is, that point where you are willing to take one of the alternatives you have. This could be staying with your current employer or taking another offer. But you may have long-term aspirations that the experience you will gain in this job will help you achieve much more than your alternatives. Do not just focus on short-term financial gains, but on your long-term career goals.

In my role I negotiate with both job candidates and potential employers. When I go into a negotiation, I know what the appropriate parameters should be because of my research and experience. I then try to understand the candidates and employers' objectives. This is the same approach that you should take in order to increase your success in your next negotiation.

Over the years I have spoken with hiring managers and other recruiters about their experiences and opinions on salary negotiations. None of them are offended when a candidate makes a counteroffer, as long as it is done well.

Universally, we do not like candidates to play negotiation games. You would be wise to avoid the terrible hardball negotiation advice out there. Remember, you are not haggling with a street vendor or a used car salesman, you are negotiating with your potential employer. There is a relationship to consider and being collaborative in your negotiations will benefit that relationship. I can almost see the defensive reaction that either side takes when they feel that the other is playing games.

You will be far more successful at negotiating if you are trying to accomplish your own goals while also trying to provide solutions to the other sides' goals. The most impactful step that you can take to make your salary negotiations more successful is to **ASK**, because most of you do not.

If you found this book to be valuable, please remember to leave a review to let others know.

About the Author

M.L. Miller was born in Washington state, grew up in Oregon and, having lived in various places around the United States, he is now back living in a small coastal town in the Pacific Northwest with his wife Wilawan.

Having studied Economics/Finance at the University of Hartford in Connecticut, M.L. began a career in recruitment in 1997, working for hundreds of client companies from Fortune 100 large companies to start ups. During this time, he has conducted somewhere between twenty and thirty thousand job interviews and has hired thousands of employees in a variety of roles from entry-level positions to C-Suite and Board-Level. His abilities caused him to branch out to start Ethical Recruiters, Inc. and later to found SoaringME, a company that educates candidates on successful job interviewing.

Within this framework M.L. is also publishing books related to the subject and has already completed three:

- SoaringME The Ultimate Guide to Successful Job Interviewing
- SoaringME COMPANION WORKBOOK The Ultimate Guide to Successful Job Interviewing
- SoaringME.com: Guide to Successful Salary Negotiation

He has plans to write more in the future, including books that will concentrate on distinct careers.

In his free time M.L. is an avid cyclist and has ridden the annual 200-mile Seattle-to-Portland bike ride five times so far. He also enjoys traveling domestically and internationally.

M.L likes to give something back to society and has worked with homeless military veterans for a couple of years through a non-profit organization. He used his experience to help them improve interviewing skills, write resumes, and obtain employment to get back on their feet. He also raises money for children's mental health charities.

In the future M.L. wants to continue with his successful business interests, while helping others achieve their dreams. He would one day like to combine his love of cycling and travel and complete a 100-mile bike ride on five different continents.

Made in United States
Orlando, FL
11 January 2023

28559912R00036